CREDIT REPAIR IN AMERICA

A REFERENCE TEXT ON HOW TO REPAIR YOUR CREDIT RATING

BY WILLIAM COLUCCI

TABLE OF CONTENTS

SECTION   No.

INTRODUCTION   1

FIRST LET US DEFINE CREDIT   2

WHY IS GOOD CREDIT NECESSARY?   3

WHAT IS A CREDIT REPORTING
AGENCY?   4

MAJOR CREDIT BUREAUS   5

    EQUIFAX   5a.
    EXPERIAN   5b.
    TRANSUNION   5c.

WHEN CREDIT IS DENIED TO YOU,
KNOW YOUR RIGHTS   6

WHAT IS A CREDIT FILE?   7

HOW TO OBTAIN A COPY OF YOUR
CREDIT REPORT   8

HOW DOES INFORMATION GET ON A
CREDIT FILE   9

CHECK YOUR OWN FILES REGULARLY
AS MISTAKES DO HAPPEN   10

FACTS TAKEN INTO CONSIDERATION
BY CREDIT GRANTERS BESIDES YOUR
CREDIT REPORT   11

BANK RECORDS   11.1

EMPLOYMENT   11.2

RESIDENCE   11.3

THE FAIR CREDIT REPORTING ACT   12

INVESTIGATIVE CONSUMER REPORT 13

DISPUTING YOUR CREDIT REPORT   14

REPORT AN ERROR BY A
COLLECTION AGENCY   15

IF THERE ARE TWO OR MORE
LISTINGS OF THE SAME
ACCOUNT   15.1

UNAUTHORIZED INQUIRIES   15.2

JUDGEMENT   15.3

SATISFIED JUDGEMENT   15.4

TAX LIEN   15.5

INCORRECT RECORDING OF A
BANKRUPTCY IN YOUR NAME   15.6

ACCOUNT CHARGED OFF
BY CREDITOR   15.7

AN INQUIRY THAT RESULTS IN A
NEW ACCOUNT BEING OPENED   15.8

SAMPLE OF A DISPUTE DIRECTLY
WITH A CREDITOR   16

SAMPLE LETTER PERTAINING TO
INCORRECT CREDIT INFORMATION   16.1

SAMPLE LETTER IF THERE WAS A
NEGATIVE REPORT FILED DUE TO
YOU'RE HAVING A DISPUTE WITH
THE CREDITOR OVER BILLING,
SHIPPING, ETC.   16.2

NEGOTIATE WITHA CREDITOR FOR
THEM TO REMOVE NEGATIVE ITEMS
FROM YOUR ACCOUNT IN
EXCHANGE   FOR REPAYMENT   16.3

SEND A FOLLOW UP LETTER THREE
OR FOUR WEEKS AFTER A DISPUTE
LETTER, THREE TO SIX WEEKS AFTER
THE FIRST LETTER   16.4

SAMPLE FOLLOW UP LETTER   17

DISPUTE A CREDIT PROBLEM BY
DEALING DIRECTLY WITH THE
CREDITOR   18

NEGOTIATE WITH CREDITORS   19

IF YOUR CREDIT FILE IS CLOSED   20

LEGAL ACTION   21

NEGOTIATE WITH A CREDITOR
BEFORE A REPORT GOES IN AND
LIMIIT DAMAGE   22

WHAT IS A CONSUMER STATEMENT
AND HOW IT BENEFITS YOU   23

FLOW CHART No. 1
CREDIT CORRECTION FLOW CHART 24

FLOW CHART No. 2
DISPUTING A CREDIT REPORT   25

PART II - REBUILDING CREDIT
ALL ABOUT LOANS   26

FINANCE COMPANIES   27

LEASE TO OWN   28

CAR AND LIGHT TRUCK
LEASORS OF LAST RESORT   29

A DIFFERENT KIND OF LOAN
APPLICATION TECHNIQUE   30

IMPORTANCE OF CREDIT CARDS   31

TYPES OF CREDIT CARDS   32

      NORMAL   32.1
      SUPPLEMENTARY   32.2
      CO-SIGNED   32.3
      SECURED   32.4
      CAMPAIGN   32.5

FINANCE COMPANIES   33

CAR AND TRUCK FINANCING   34

LOAN GRANTING CRITERIA   35

NEGATIVE ITEMS ON A CREDIT
APPLICATION   36

IDENTITY THEFT   37

PARTING NOTES   38

QUESTIONS ON CREDIT
REPAIR CYCLE   39

ANSWERS TO QUESTIONS   40

1. INTRODUCTION

As of July 28, 2010, the "Total Public Debt Outstanding" (in the entire U.S.A.) was approximately 93% of annual GDP, ($13.258 Trillion) with the constituent parts of the debt being "Debt held by the Public" being approximately 60% of GDP ($8.63 Trillion) and "Intergovernmental Debt" standing at 32% of GDP ($4.55 Trillion).

You need to be aware that the files that are out there with your personal credit information may be in error. If they are, no one will ever know or do anything about it unless **YOU** take the appropriate steps. I want to help you take those steps and that is what this book is for. This book is NOT to assist anyone in avoiding paying their debts. Ultimately, if you wish to purchase something, be prepared to pay for it. If you sign a contract, be prepared to live within the terms of that contract. Nonetheless, we all make mistakes and can go through hard times. This book will help those earnest and honest people who wish to repair a bad credit history and regain the invaluable use of good credit.

Credit Bureaus do not correct erroneous or incomplete information on credit files unless someone complains and even then, it requires some effort to prod them along.

The VantageScore system now used by Equifax, Experian and Transunion has brought a degree of similarity to credit scoring. Nonetheless, it is extremely likely that the sourced information used by the three rating companies will not be identical. This could explain why credit scores for the same individual can vary amongst the three major credit bureaus.

The VantageScore system rates the consumer between 501 and 990 (according to Transunion). The levels of score are as follows:

A: 901 – 990
B: 801 – 900
C: 701 – 800
D: 601 – 700
F: 501 – 600

The VantageScore system breaks down many characteristics that make us better or worse credit risks and the different area of credit history are weighted differently.

Category	Description	Weight
Payment History	How timely and consistent your payments are	32%
Credit Utilization	Debt-to-credit ratios and how much credit is available	23%
Credit Balances	What your total debt is: most likely, delinquent debt is counted more harshly than current debt	15%
Depth of Credit	Length of credit history	13%
Recent Credit	How recent and how many new hard inquiries and new account there are	10%
Available Credit	How much credit can be accessed, for example, could you spend $50,000 of credit tonight or within the next week	7%

Since lenders also look at debt to income ratio, someone who pays all bills, but has a limited income is viewed well, but not at the best risk level.

Matters such as cheques returned "Not Sufficient Funds" (NSF) or late payments, will be taken into consideration and viewed as negatives. Late payments are further classified as 30, 60 or 90 days late. Unfortunately, the lenders don't care if you were ill or out of work for a short period of time, and it is their job to judge us exclusively on our history of paying bills.

There are a lot of credit repair firms springing up all around and they may not be what they promise to be for the person wanting to correct his or her poor credit situation. If there is inaccurate information posted at one of the three major credit reporting services, contact Equifax, Transunion and/or Experian and ask them in writing to correct the errors. Any person or organization who has denied you credit based on a credit report must tell you if a credit report was used for the decision and from which agency the information came from.

LINKS TO MAJOR CREDIT AGENCIES

EQUIFAX
http://www.equifax.com
TRANSUNION
http://www.transunion.com
EXPERIAN
http://www.experian.com

(or just search "Equifax.com") and you can presently obtain a free copy of your credit report based on a 30 day trial offer.

Your credit report starts when you first begin buying on credit and it is usually updated every 30 days. According to Equifax, of those Americans denied credit due to credit reports, most believe there were inaccuracies in the credit files.

Please read on and learn how to correct your credit rating.

2. FIRST, LET US DEFINE CREDIT

From the farmer who must mortgage his land in faith of the coming harvest, to the businessman who risks mortgaging everything to expand in hopes of capturing new markets, we use, employ, corrupt, rely upon, abuse, and are saved by credit more and more each and every year.

Simply spoken, as we most commonly use it and as this book deals with it, credit is a promise to pay back money at a later date, usually with interest.

There are several reasons why you may be denied a loan, they include:

- If you do not live in the USA or an American territory;
- If you have declared bankruptcy;
- If you have continuously bounced checks;
- If you have no credit history or have a low credit score;
- If you have had difficulty making payments or have had a repossession of a vehicle or property.

3. WHY IS GOOD CREDIT NECESSARY? (As if you didn't know!)

Whether we need credit as much as the farmer who depends upon it to purchase seed, or if we would like credit for something as simple as convenience, is only a matter of private concern. Credit is a necessity in our society and to live without credit you must be either tremendously wealthy or destitute.

You require good credit to arrange a mortgage, purchase a house, a car, or for acceptance to many jobs. It has been known to affect peoples standing in the community and acceptance to clubs and other social groups as well.

Credit will, of course affect your eligibility for credit cards and it is extremely difficult to rent a car, make a hotel reservation or purchase an airline ticket without a credit card. To say nothing of the convenience and the safety net in case of emergencies.

Without good credit, as I am sure many readers are aware, life suffers, however, there are things that you can do to improve damaged credit ratings and in some cases terrible reports can be completely repaired.

Please read on.

4. WHAT IS A CREDIT REPORTING AGENCY?

A credit reporting agency or credit bureau as they are often known as is in business to sell credit information on people, other businesses or both for profit. They are not a government institution and they are definitely not beyond human or computer error in the correlating and compiling of information on the millions of individuals and accounts they document each year.

5. MAJOR CREDIT BUREAUS

5a. EQUIFAX

http://www.equifax.com

By far, the largest credit reporting bureau in America, if not in the world, is Equifax. Equifax has files on over four hundred million lines of credit and you are probably one of them. It used to be a challenge dealing with the reporting firms; however, since the Internet this is one place in our lives that functions better.

5b. EXPERIAN

http://www.experian.com

Formerly known as CNN Systems, Experian has operations in 36 countries and has global reach.

5c. TRANSUNION

http://www.transunion.com

Created in 1968 and formerly

known as Union Tank Car Company, TransUnion has grown to be the third largest Credit Bureau in the U.S.A.

An unrealistic number of Americans have found inaccuracies in their credit files. These may not be the fault of the credit reporting agency as administrators in lending institutions who report information to the agencies are also human and therefore subject to human error. When I researched, I discovered that Equifax was by far the largest credit bureau in my area and that they would have the most complete files available on individual citizens.

When denied credit, you have the right to be told if a credit report was used in making the decision to deny you credit and which credit bureau a report was obtained from.

6. WHEN CREDIT IS DENIED TO YOU-- KNOW YOUR RIGHTS!

After learning what credit bureau has a negative file on you, you should obtain a copy of your credit report from the bureau involved. The easiest way to do this is from their web site. The other method for those without the use of a computer is to write a letter to the credit bureau. If you discover there was an issue worthy of discussion, write them a letter, and include in it:

1) Your name;
2) Your address;
3) Your previous address;
4) Your present & previous Employers;
5) Your social security number (only if you wish to.);
6) Your date of birth.

The agency would also like your spouse's name, although this could prove to be an inconvenience later on.

In your communication, simply request your credit file from them. This is a right supported by the Fair Credit Act and will be your main weapon in fighting bad credit.

7. WHAT IS A CREDIT FILE?

A credit file is the total file the credit bureau has on an individual or company. These are guarded jealously and are the "product" that the credit bureau markets. In order to keep business neat and mailing and communications under control the credit bureau actually sells encapsulated neat little packages or *credit reports* which tell your credit worthiness in the easiest and most simple way.

In order to understand the likelihood of your paying back loans, the lenders rely on your *Credit Score* which is stored in your *Credit Report* at the *Credit Reporting Agency*.

Terms and conditions for loans vary between lenders; therefore, they can and usually will interpret the information based on their own policies. Different lenders set their own policies and evaluations of risk and there is no firm line between good and bad credit or good and bad risk.

The credit bureau has no control over the policies of individual lenders or other reporting companies. Several types of businesses send reports to the credit reporting agency, including: banks, finance companies, auto leasing companies, credit card companies, credit unions and some retailers. Other records come from courthouses across the country and from collection agencies.

When considering whether to grant a mortgage, the lender will consider the value and condition of the property, the homeowner's equity, the size of the down payment, their relationship with the client (do you have other financial services with that lender?), and any other debts. It is to their benefit for you to understand the process they use to grant or refuse credit.

What lenders are looking for in your credit score is the likelihood that you will pay them back regularly and consistently and they get an idea of that from your credit score. They do not care about your gender or your race, they are in the business of lending money, however they want to lend the money to people who can and will pay them back with interest. The interest is, after all, their profit. No loan, no profit!

These credit reports are made available to members of the credit reporting agencies, who in turn pay for this service. This service is important to the credit industry, so important, that this private information is available on almost all of us and is controlled by *The Fair Credit Act*.

Your credit score should contain an accurate, although possibly not all inclusive, background of your past credit transactions. To create the credit report, the Credit Reporting Agency looks at your past payment behavior, the amount of your debt and how it compares to your income plus the history of past debts and payments.

A high credit score would be seen as favorable when considering you for loans. A credit score that is high would receive small impact from one or two negative comments or items, likewise, a low credit score would have little impact from one or two positive coments.

You can disagree with your credit report and dispute an item and the credit reporting agency should invesgitate it in order to verify its accuracy. While the item is in dispute, it would not be listed on your credit report.

Credit information is collected daily and can change your credit score from one day to the next. Although mortgage information may appear on your credit report, it is not calculated into your credit score.

8.   HOW TO OBTAIN A COPY OF YOUR CREDIT REPORT

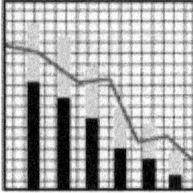

Section 609 of the Fair Credit Act provides you with the authority to access your own credit file information in the form of a credit report.

Go to the email address:
www.AnnualCreditReport.com

This web site is sponsored by Transunion, Experian and Equifax to provide you with a copy of your credit report for free once per year.

You should have available:

- full name;
- current billing address;
- your previous address;
- your email address;
- telephone numbers.

What you will receive back from the credit bureau will be several pages of your credit history stretching back several years. The deciphering of the new format of a credit report should be fairly straight forward, just don't expect to be recognized for having done something right, if any credit bureau reported only good things to its members it would soon lose its justification for existence.

Most transactions automatically purge from the system after three years; although this is neither an official habit nor guaranteed. If you dispute an item you can, as mentioned earlier, ask for a review of the item, dispute its accuracy or include a comment on your file in your own words. Judgments, seizures of property, garnishment of wages and all fixed loans automatically purge from the system after six years.

In order to maintain a good credit file:

- Make all bill payments on time;
- Keep your account balances below 75% of their maximum;
- Don't apply for credit unless you have a real need for it. Frivolous inquiries damage your credit score and may suggest you may be open to too much debt.

Individuals are not permitted access to credit files of others and businesses require a legitimate reason for accessing credit information as well. When you apply for a loan or a credit card, you are normally asked to sign a form permitting them access to your credit file and it is this form that permits them to obtain private information on you. You do not have to sign the form; however, you may jeopardize your chances of obtaining credit if you do not sign it as anykone accessing your credit file must comply with the strict laws controlling this industry.

You may wonder what some information on applications has to do with the application's purpose. The credit reporting agencies use such information as your date of birth, present and previous addresses and perhaps employer information to confirm your identity and to make sure they are releasing the proper information on the correct individual. Even with all these checks and confirmations, errors do occur. If they did not conduct these checks there would be significantly more likelihood of error. Every request for access to your credit file is reported in the file. When you are turned down for credit you have the right   to obtain the name of the credit reporting agency used for the decision (if one was used).

You can then check your own credit report and review the information objectively. This will help you take the necessary steps to correct your credit report and improve your credit worthiness, subsequently improving your lifestyle. Remember that the credit reporting agency may have a disclaimer on their web site or personal report that they are not responsible for errors or omissions.

There are only certain acceptable reasons for which the credit reporting agency will release your credit information. They are as follows:

- Credit (whether a loan or a credit card);
- Collections;
- Housing rental;
- Employment;
- Insurance;
- Other lenders;
- Utility Cos.;
- Court Orders(to evaluate credit behavior).

Neither Equifax, Experian nor TransUnion will sell trade or rent your personal information. You will never receive advertisements or junk mail that has used the credit reporting agency's database in order to target you. They can, however, use your personal information to contact you themselves for their own promotions and services. This is a service, though, that you can ask to be omitted from. If you do not want your personal information used for marketing you should contact the agencies to ensure that you are removed from their list.

As well, credit agencies will supply personal information if a subpoena, search warrant or court order requires them to do so.

9. HOW DOES INFORMATION GET ON A CREDIT FILE?

 A credit bureau has two main jobs to perform if it wishes to sell credit reports. As we have covered, it sells credit reports on individuals and businesses; however, first it must compile available information on these people or companies in order to have a product to sell. Traditionally, there are certain types of businesses that report back to the credit bureaus and certain types that do not.

We cannot assume who will and who will not report information back to the credit bureaus., but typically some small businesses do not typically go through the trouble, although large companies who belong to a credit bureau almost always report credit information.

Those financial institutions which usually do not report all transactions will often report some negative information. If you apply for a mortgage, the mortgage company will often ask for reports from the non-reporting organizations. If you pay your small loan off promptly every month, it will never appear on your credit report, however, if you miss a payment this negative information will become available to any bureau member who purchases your credit report. This is another example of how the credit reporting system tends to give more negative than positive information. There are, however; limitations as to what the credit bureaus can legally include in your credit file and add to your credit report. Please refer to Section 604 of the Fair Credit Reporting Act for those limitations as they are quite involved. The restrictions include medical information but there are several caveats and exceptions to all information. There are special provisions for national security, a request from a head of State or local child support enforcement agencies.

For your copy of the Fair Credit Reporting Act on computer or to print it out, please go to:

http://www.ftc.gov/os/statutes/031224fcra.pdf

Credit bureaus also tend to try to keep their files fairly updated and usually they will automatically remove late payments in three years or less. Accounts closed by creditors and bankruptcies will usually remain on your file for at least seven years.

10. CHECK YOUR OWN FILES REGULARLY AS MISTAKES HAPPEN

It is becoming increasingly common for illegal aliens and/or criminals to obtain and use someone else's Social Security Number without their knowledge or consent. Sometimes they will use your name as well. With today's technology, it is easy to manufacture a reasonable copy of your driver's license or other I.D. and your credit history may reflect someone else's purchases. Your best defence against this is to check you credit file often. New laws are helping to protect the consumer against identity theft; however the criminals can adapt quickly to opportunity. **Be careful!**

11. FACTS TAKEN INTO CONSIDERATION BY CREDIT GRANTERS BESIDES YOUR CREDIT REPORT

There are a few important points to remember regarding your credit file and the resulting credit report.

The Fair Credit Reporting Act indicates that most information stays in your credit report for up to seveh years.

Some information may be deleted prior to seven years; however, often the information that it is most damaging remains on file for the full term. Also remember that the seven years starts to be counted whenever there is activity on the specific item.

- If you go bankrupt, this will appear on your report for up to 10 years.

- If you have had a lawsuit or an unpaid judgment this can appear on your report for seven years unless the statute of limitations ends. Whichever is longer will take precedence.

- Information regarding an application for more than $150,000 of credit or life insurance has no time limit

- An application for a job paying more than $75,000 has no time limit

- There is no time limit to report a criminal conviction

11.1   BANK RECORDS

Credit granters consider more than just your credit rating when making the decision whether to grant you credit or not. They will also take into consideration your bank record.

You may recall applying for credit and being asked to write down your bank address. The credit granter would take that piece of information, contact your bank and ask them how many N.S.F. cheques you have written in the past year, or perhaps they may go back even further. Every N.S.F. cheque someone writes is a testimony to their inability to pay, or other even worse habits. If you have written too many N.S.F. cheques, for any reason (I know accidents happen, but I don't count) your best defence is to simply change banks and don't give your old bank as a reference.

Creditors don't usually have the resources or the inclination to check every bank in town to see if they know you, you just aren't that important to them (sorry). Once you have established yourself as an upstanding customer of the new bank take precautions! Try to maintain a minimum balance in your chequing account so as to have a cushion in case of slip ups, or get overdraft protection, it costs when you use it but it may be worth it.

11.2　EMPLOYMENT

Creditors like people who are very, very boring! If you mined for gold in the Amazon for the past twenty years and recently retired here with two million dollars in cash that is good, because credit will be difficult to obtain.

Credit granters like to see solid, consistent habits in the people they grant credit to. Two or more years of continuous employment looks very good to a loans officer. Consistency of employment and good repayment habits are <u>much</u> more important to these people than your total income is. Just think for a moment, some people earn $30,000. per year and make all the payments on their sixty thousand dollar car, while some others earn $120,000 and can't make their regular payments on a $25,000 vehicle. Where you work matters, but not much, what you do matters, but not much. What matters is that you work and have been working for at least two years for the same company. Variety or experience doesn't help, consistency does!

Some lenders consider self employed individuals a greater risk than salaried employees. The roller coaster ride of sales or the seasonal character of many sole proprietorships make them less attractive to credit granters. To work around this problem, consider making yourself an employee of your small company. Make yourself "Manager of Joe's Plumbing" or "President of Lisa's Catering". This is easy to set up by drawing a salary against your own small business.

11.3   RESIDENCE

The last thing the credit granter or loans officer will look at is the length of time you have been at your present address and were at your previous address. Yes, it is that word again, consistency! If you were to loan someone money or sell them something on credit wouldn't you like to know if they are in the habit of disappearing? Again, at least two years at one location looks good, ten years looks great.

12.   FAIR CREDIT REPORTING ACT

You do have rights with regards to your credit and

the reporting of information regarding your credit. These rights are outlined thoroughly in the "FAIR CREDIT REPORTING ACT", and knowledge of this Act will be a valuable tool in correcting your credit rating and protecting yourself from misuse of your credit information. Many important rights are dealt with in this act, including:

    i. How long a bankruptcy can remain on your credit file?

    ii. How long a judgement can remain on your credit file?

    iii. Your rights to access your own credit file?

    iv. Your rights to receive assistance from the reporting agency assuring that only the most recent and most reliable information is on your credit file?

    v. Who has legal access to your credit report?

vi. What information can legally be included in your credit file?

13. INVESTIGATIVE CONSUMER REPORT

They have to tell you when they have conducted an Investigative Consumer Report on you. Please refer to section 606 of the FAIR CREDIT REPORTING ACT.

"Disclosure of investigative consumer reports
[15 U.S.C. x 1681d]

(a) Disclosure of fact of preparation. A person may not procure or cause to be prepared an investigative consumer report on any consumer unless

    (1)   it is clearly and accurately disclosed to the consumer that an investigative consumer report including information as to his character, general reputation, personal characteristics mode of living, whichever are applicable,

34

may be made, and such disclosure

(a) is made in a writing mailed, or otherwise delivered, to the consumer, not later than three days after the date on which the report was first requested, and

(b) includes a statement informing the consumer of his right to request the additional disclosures provided for under subsection (b) of this section and the written summary of the rights of the consumer prepared pursuant to section 609(c) [s 1681g]; and

(2) the person certifies or has certified to the consumer reporting agency that

(a) the person has made the disclosures to the consumer required by paragraph (1);

(b) *the*
person will comply
with subsection (b).

The government has been kind enough to supply you with the facilities to correct or amend your credit files by using the reporting bureaus resources and personnel. Don't be hesitant; you may be surprised at how helpful these people can be.

14. DISPUTING YOUR CREDIT REPORT

The first step, as it has been outlined is to obtain your credit file, determine the items with which you disagree or which you would like to challenge. Be sure that you have some grounds for challenging all the items that you isolate, as frivolous requests will quickly earn you a form letter telling you that you are proceeding frivolously and as a result the agency will not proceed. Mail or email only three or fewer items at a time, be courteous and don't be too proud to rely upon their advice and expertise. Don't despair if you receive a letter saying your request or submission is frivolous. Keep notes on the dates of your mailing and send a follow up letter two to three weeks later. If your follow up letter receives a reply that they never received your first letter then remail your request for help and this time send it by registered mail and keep the receipt. Better yet, spend the extra money and register the letter "return receipt requested", that way you can prove if the agency received your letter and you will have the name of the person who signed for it.

Your dispute must tell **WHAT** you want investigated and it must tell **WHY** it requires investigation. Be very specific, be very accurate, document dates, companies, items (purchases, amounts etc.), send photocopies of cancelled cheques if possible. List amounts as detailed as possible, relay which things related to the particular item are true and which are false, mistaken or in error. Keep careful notes. If you are unhappy with the results of the investigation, don't give up, learn where your weaknesses are, try using the address of a friend out of town and send an improved request to the credit bureau in his/her municipality. If you are successful in correcting items on your report wait a couple of weeks and try correcting a few more items.

Remember the following:

- Don't use a letterhead;

- Go for humility, not bravado. If they think you are some slick character they are not going to be very helpful. If you can establish a rapport you will do better, so be nice, even if the person you are dealing with is not;

- Write your letters in simple language, they are there to help John Doe, not some slick, deadbeat millionaire;

- If you can get a dispute form from the bureau, use it;

- Keep copies of all correspondence;

  Remember the order:

  (1) Send in one dispute letter for three or less items;

  (2) Wait four weeks;

  (3) Send a follow up letter;

  (4) Either re-mail (or email)

a dispute letter or calmly wait for action on your dispute (no more than seven weeks).

Your opinion is valid. The Equifax website even offers this helpful advice:

"You may include a brief written statement in your credit file to be included on any future credit report."

15. REPORTING AN ERROR BY A COLLECTION AGENCY

"The records as per my credit report from company ABC are incorrect. I do not owe money to this company. Please investigate this account and verify any alleged connection to me. If your investigation shows any connection to me, please inform me of the name of the person from whom the information originates, so I can contact them personally to correct this misunderstanding."

15.1 IF THERE ARE TWO OR MORE LISTINGS OF THE SAME ACCOUNT

"I have never had two (or three) accounts with this bank (or company). It appears your information is in error. Please investigate and correct this as soon as possible."

(In this instance you know the company originating the item so it would be easy for you to follow up yourself should the agency be unwilling or still receives erroneous information. However, it is always easier to allow the agency to correct these things on your bahalf, when possible.)

15.2 UNAUTHORIZED INQUIRIES

"This inquiry was not authorized by me. I do not

know this person nor have I authorized this inquiry. Please remove this inquiry from my report immediately and forward to me the name of the person who requested information on my report."

15.3 JUDGEMENT

"There is a mistake. I was never served with this lawsuit. Please conduct a more thorough investigation and remove this judgement from my report."

(Try using this if you have never been served with the judgement or did not attend the court proceedings and had a default judgement issued.)

15.4 SATISFIED JUDGEMENT

"This judgement has been satisfied. Please verify this with the creditor and remove it from my credit report."

(This will work best if (1) the creditor is no longer in business (2) if it has been two or three years since the judgement or (3) if it is difficult to locate the creditor to verify the information.)

Having a judgement set aside may be beyond the ability of even the most able amateur, if this is part of your problem you might do well to contact a professional

15.5. TAX LIEN

"This tax lien was fully paid on (date), please verify and update my credit file to reflect the present situation."

15.6 INCORRECT RECORDING OF A BANKRUPTCY IN YOUR NAME

"I have never declared bankruptcy. The amount of *(amount)* attributed to me on *(Date)* is not true. Please investigate this and remove it from my report."

15.7 ACCOUNT CHARGED OFF BY CREDITOR

"I have never had an account with *(name of creditor)* charged off to the amount of *(amount)*. Please investigate and correct my account to reflect this. If you find you are unable to remove this charge from my account please inform me of the name of the person or company from whom this information originates so I may satisfy my debts or correct outstanding errors."

15.8 AN INQUIRY THAT RESULTS IN A NEW ACCOUNT BEING OPENED

"The inquiry on my credit file by *(name of creditor)* resulted in opening an account with that company. The manner in which you have presented this material is misleading and does not reflect the truth. Please remove this inquiry so as to better present the truth."

16. SAMPLE OF A DISPUTE DIRECTLY WITH A CREDITOR

"You have billed me for (item) which I did not receive. I have paid you for every item that I have received; however, I do not feel obliged to pay for something that I did not receive. Please stop harassing me for payment, or I will hand this matter over to my attorney and you can deal with him in court."

16.1 SAMPLE OF A LETTER PERTAINING TO INCORRECT CREDIT INFORMATION

"A credit report recently supplied to me by (name of credit bureau) shows that I owe you (amount) ..."

"shows that I paid you late (number of times)..."

"shows that I failed to make (number of payments)..."

"..This is not accurate. My records indicate that I always paid my account promptly and as agreed. The report that you have turned over to the credit bureau is highly injurious to my credit rating and I would like it either verified or removed immediately. Please notify (name of credit bureau) immediately of your error so that my credit rating can be spared any further damage. If the information cannot be verified please inform the credit bureau immediately so that it can be removed promptly from my credit rating."

(Send photocopies of cancelled cheques or other proof of payments, this will assist in obtaining a correction on your account.)

"Your prompt attention to this matter and a response will be appreciated and may help me to avoid legal action.

Yours truly,"
(your name)

16.2 SAMPLE LETTER IF THERE WAS A NEGATIVE REPORT FILED DUE TO YOUR HAVING A DISPUTE WITH THE CREDITOR OVER BILLING, SHIPPING, ETC.

"Reports obtained from (name of credit bureau) show that my account with your company, account number ...., was paid .... days late, ... times. This account was under dispute at the time due to (items short shipped, wrongly shipped, it was never shipped, it was billed incorrectly, etc.).

At the time of the dispute I contacted your billing department and was assured that there would be no problem of my being billed for the items under dispute until the dispute was resolved. The problem was resolved to my satisfaction and I hope to yours; however, I have had my credit file prejudiced by your turning in a negative report on our business transaction. My credit file has been damaged severely due to this report.

I hope you can assist me by quickly correcting this erroneous information since I do not wish to contact my lawyer over a matter which can very easily be corrected."

(Include photocopies of correspondence or at least dates of telephone calls and the name(s) of the person(s) with whom you have spoken. For future reference, remember that written correspondence is more powerful in a dispute. If your skill at writing in English is limited, ask a friend with good writing skills to help you.)

16.3 IF YOU WANT TO NEGOTIATE WITH THE CREDITOR FOR THEM TO REMOVE NEGATIVE ITEMS FROM YOUR ACCOUNT IN EXCHANGE FOR REPAYMENT

"I wish to confirm our telephone conversation on (date), regarding the settlement of account *(account detail)."*

"As agreed, I will pay to your company the amount of $......., as full settlement for this account."

"On behalf of (name of company) you have agreed, upon receipt of this money, to (change, delete, paid satisfactory, etc.) my credit report."

"I appreciate your cooperation in this matter and will forward a cheque to you in the agreed amount as soon as a completed, signed copy of this letter is returned to me.

Thank you very much for your assistance in this matter.

_____
(Signature of authorized person)

For:_____
(Name of company)

Date:_____

16.4 SEND A FOLLOW UP LETTER THREE OR FOUR WEEKS AFTER A DISPUTE LETTER AND THREE TO SIX WEEKS AFTER THE FIRST LETTER

17. SAMPLE FOLLOW UP LETTER

Date
On (*Date of dispute letter*), I sent you a letter requesting that you investigate certain items on my credit file that I believe to be inaccurate.

I have not yet received either a response or an acknowledgement of my letter and six weeks have passed since I mailed it to you.

I would anticipate an investigation within a reasonable time and I believe a reasonable time has passed.

If you cannot verify the information as outlined in the enclosed copy of my letter would you please delete these items from my credit file? Please respond immediately to this matter as it is now overdue.

I await your response and immediate attention.

Yours truly,
(your name)

18. DISPUTE A CREDIT PROBLEM BY DEALING DIRECTLY WITH THE CREDITOR

It is true that bad credit can affect your credit rating for up to seven years and in some instances ten years (F.C.R.A. s 609) although that does **not** mean that it **always** has to be so. Aside from bankruptcy, many other credit problems can be corrected or improved in less than seven years.

Even without you doing anything at all ,your credit rating will start to be purged of most old information after 24 to 36 months.

Credit bureaus and creditors try to keep their files relatively recent and that is the reason for the purging. The time may vary from bureau to bureau or creditor to creditor, but few can afford to allow their files to grow stale through neglect.

If you challenge a statement on your credit file that is 36 months old, the bureau could have difficulty in verifying such an old item. If the bureau has no record of a bad account under your name you are home free; if the bureau has a record of a bad account or an account paid 60 or 90 days late, you can insist that they attempt to verify it through the creditor. If the creditor has already purged his records, there is little chance of his confirming the bad history to the bureau. Again, you are home free.

Although not always necessary, you might wish to check to see if a particular debt has been purged by a particular creditor before proceeding to challenge it with the credit bureau. Verifying such items is fairly simple to do. Simply write or telephone the

creditor and ask them if they can verify
such information. It is usually a good idea
to carry out this qualifying of borderline
accounts before going ahead to challenge
the next generation of problems through
the credit bureau. This will parmit you to
be as effective as possible in correcting the
three or four accounts that you send to the
credit bureau for them to assist you in
verifying and hopefully correcting.

19. NEGOTIATE WITH CREDITORS

In correcting a credit file there is always the
opportunity to negotiate directly with the
creditor, because after all, it is the creditor
who initiated the damaging comment
before it ever got on your credit file.

The main point to remember when
approaching a creditor to improve or delete
a comment initiated by them is that
anything can be negotiated. If the creditor
still has an outstanding debt in your name,
ask if they will accept partial payment in
exchange for removing the negative
comment they gave to the credit bureau on
you. Remember, most creditors are
motivated by the bottom line, they aren't
after blood, and all they are interested in is
getting their money.

Be prepared for "no way", "no deal" and "we will not budge". This is where your negotiating skills come in. If your telephone conversation is less than a minute in length you must try harder. Make notes on your strategy prior to the telephone call or writing a letter, refer to your notes and approach the negotiation in an objective, businesslike manner. After all, to the creditor it is business, even when it is personal to you.

Approach a creditor with the offer to pay all or part of the debt in exchange for their removing the damaging comment. If they are at all receptive, tell them that you would like to formalize your discussion on paper, or if you approached them in writing be sure to save all correspondence and emails. Tell the creditor that once they have removed the comment from your credit file you will pay them a predetermined (in writing) amount of money immediately, and if they are in doubt as to whether you will comply, reassure them that they can always re-instate the comment if you should fail to uphold your part of the bargain, of which there is no chance whatsoever.

If the debt has already been satisfied, try approaching the creditor on humanitarian grounds. Tell them that they have nothing further to gain by damaging your credit reputation, which you are in the process of improving. Tell the creditor that you previously fell on bad times, were out of work, were ill... were a victim of recession or whichever is the truth in your particular situation. Not all but certainly some creditors will be sympathetic.

Remember always, they are paid to collect accounts, including yours. Some of these account and collections officers are very tough. They will try to force you to pay everything immediately. If you can, by all means, pay your debts. If you cannot pay the entire debt immediately, try to arrange terms. The account collection agent is by job description required to be extremely mercenary. They want money and some will say whatever they think will get them the most money the quickest. They are tough so you will have to be tough as well!

20. IF YOUR CREDIT FILE IS CLOSED GO BACK TO THE BUREAU TO INVESTIGATE

If you have paid an account off and it still shows negative remarks, go back to the credit bureau and ask them to investigate. This should not be too difficult since if the creditor no longer has an open account there is little chance of the credit bureau being able to verify any information at all. If that is the case, you should be able to get them to delete the item due to insufficient information backup or unverifiable information.

Another method you can use is to emotionally appeal to the creditor to remove the information. The creditor no longer has anything to lose by complying and might consider a good argument as viable. Thus the creditor might change a negative remark to paid, paid satisfactory or they might even agree to delete it completely.

21.   LEGAL ACTION

Consumer reporting agencies are registered under the Federal Trade Commission. It is to this Commission to whom you can direct any complaints against any of the bureaus licensed to sell credit information. Reporting complaints to the Commission will often be the easiest and most direct route to follow if you have a complaint against an agency, such as:

failing to investigate a complaint, failing to investigate a complaint within a reasonable time, or not using information that is the best available.

There may be a situation where you will require the services of a lawyer or another legal professional. The easiest first step is to consult either a lawyer or a paralegal as to the possibilities of your legal action culminating successfully. Paralegals are usually less expensive than lawyers although lawyers have certain avenues open to them that paralegals usually do not. Generally, for small claims and negotiating, paralegals are on near equal footing with lawyers and can be better for dealing with smaller amounts (and working for smaller amounts).

If you should find yourself in a situation where there is an item under dispute, your legal counsel can apply for an injunction to have the item temporarily deleted from your credit file during the legal proceedings. The law looks on it such that the item has yet to be determined true or untrue and so you cannot be expected to be encumbered by it in the meantime. The legal proceedings may not even get to court for a year or more and so you might be fifty or seventy percent of the way through the natural purge time during the delay for a court appearance.

22. NEGOTIATE WITH A CREDITOR BEFORE A REPORT GOES IN AND LIMIT DAMAGE

If you find yourself in a position where you know a negative is about to be submitted to the credit bureau against your file, don't hesitate, negotiate immediately. It is often easiest to negotiate these matters over the telephone and send follow up letters to receive any necessary signatures. It is easiest to put on a front over the telephone than in person. If you are given to emotional reactions, try to subdue them. If you have had a previous misunderstanding with a clerk or employee try to bypass them and deal with their superior. If the superior person is hostile to you remember the famous quote from Don Corleon of "The Godfather", when he said "We are both honourable men, let's discuss this problem", (or something to that effect). NEVER avoid or delay dealing with the situation; hesitation or procrastination will only make the situation worse.

If the creditor is adamant and doesn't want to negotiate, he will probably suffer a financial loss. If the creditor won't negotiate and is insistent on receiving **all** his money **immediately**, simply tell him that you are trying desperately to avoid bankruptcy, would rather pay him yourself but if he insists in forcing you into bankruptcy and he will get considerably less settlement from the trustees than what you have offered him. Offer to send post dated cheques. Be nice, but be persuasive.

23. WHAT IS A CONSUMER STATEMENT AND HOW IT BENEFITS YOU

The Fair Credit Reporting Act does allow a consumer statement and most credit bureaus support your option to do this and to add a consumer statement of up to 150 words to your credit file, and they will even help you with the wording of it. These people are not your enemies. They have a job to do and that sometimes puts us in opposition.

Your best method to proceed, after you have read your credit report and made every reasonable effort to remove derogatory remarks from your credit file, is to write the bureau a letter detailing the information that you would like to add to your file. In your letter be sure to include the same identifying information you used when requesting your report, and then, perhaps with the assistance of the bureau agent, carefully write your statement remembering specifically what you want to achieve. A consumer statement is useful in dealing with the following situations:

- If your identity is being confused with someone else's, so you can request phone verification before credit is granted, this will correct both confusion and deliberate fraud;

- To dispute a negative item that discussions with the bureau and creditors have been unable to clear up;

- To explain late or missed payments, such as illness, layoff, bereavement;

- To alert potential creditors of temporary conditions such as seasonal work shortages, return to school, etc.

The Consumer Statement can be very useful if you have had years of good credit history and suddenly find yourself with a rash of credit problems. If negotiations are under way for you to repay outstanding debts by all means include this information in your statement, it can only help.

It is regretful that omeone can commit a major crime and be free in two or three years, but if you miss a couple of payments or have a cash flow problem you might find yourself facing economic purgatory for up to seven years.

24. CREDIT CORRECTION FLOW CHART

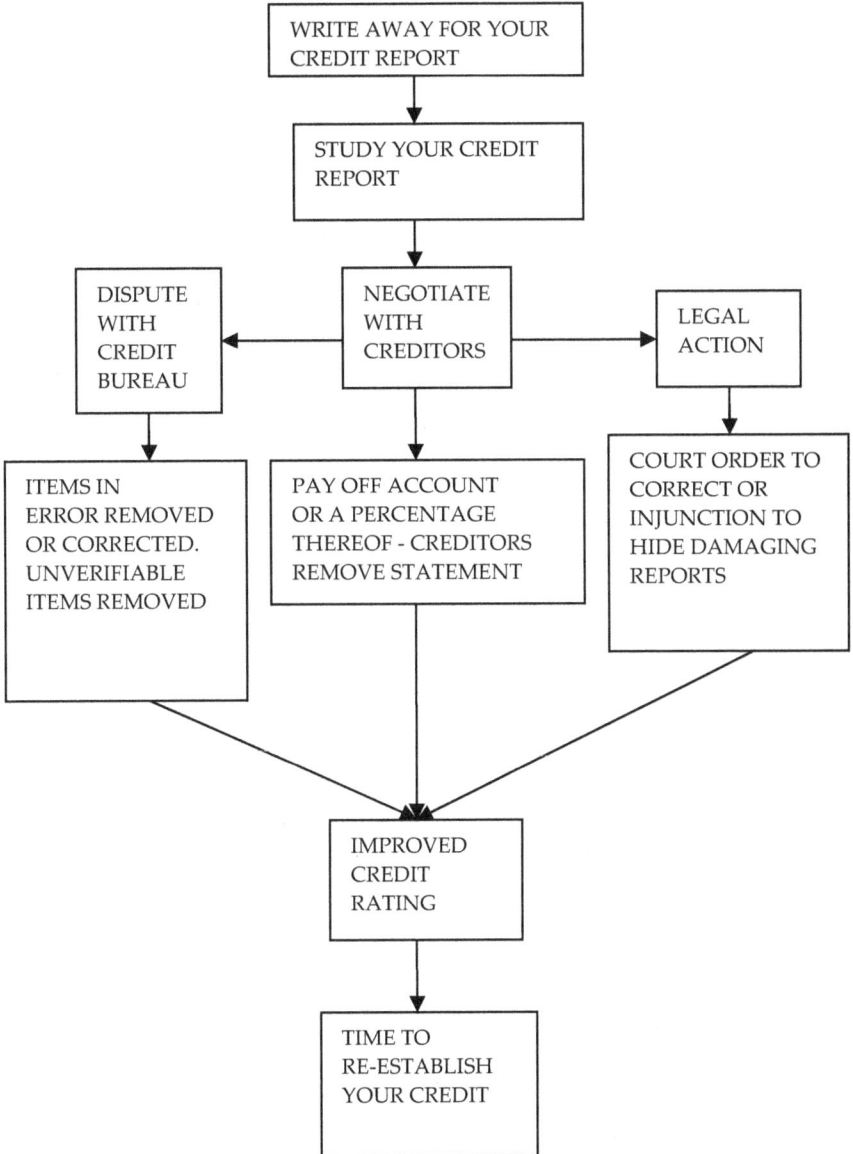

WRITE AWAY FOR YOUR CREDIT REPORT

↓

STUDY YOUR CREDIT REPORT

↓

NEGOTIATE WITH CREDITORS

← DISPUTE WITH CREDIT BUREAU

→ LEGAL ACTION

DISPUTE WITH CREDIT BUREAU → ITEMS IN ERROR REMOVED OR CORRECTED. UNVERIFIABLE ITEMS REMOVED

NEGOTIATE WITH CREDITORS → PAY OFF ACCOUNT OR A PERCENTAGE THEREOF - CREDITORS REMOVE STATEMENT

LEGAL ACTION → COURT ORDER TO CORRECT OR INJUNCTION TO HIDE DAMAGING REPORTS

↓

IMPROVED CREDIT RATING

↓

TIME TO RE-ESTABLISH YOUR CREDIT

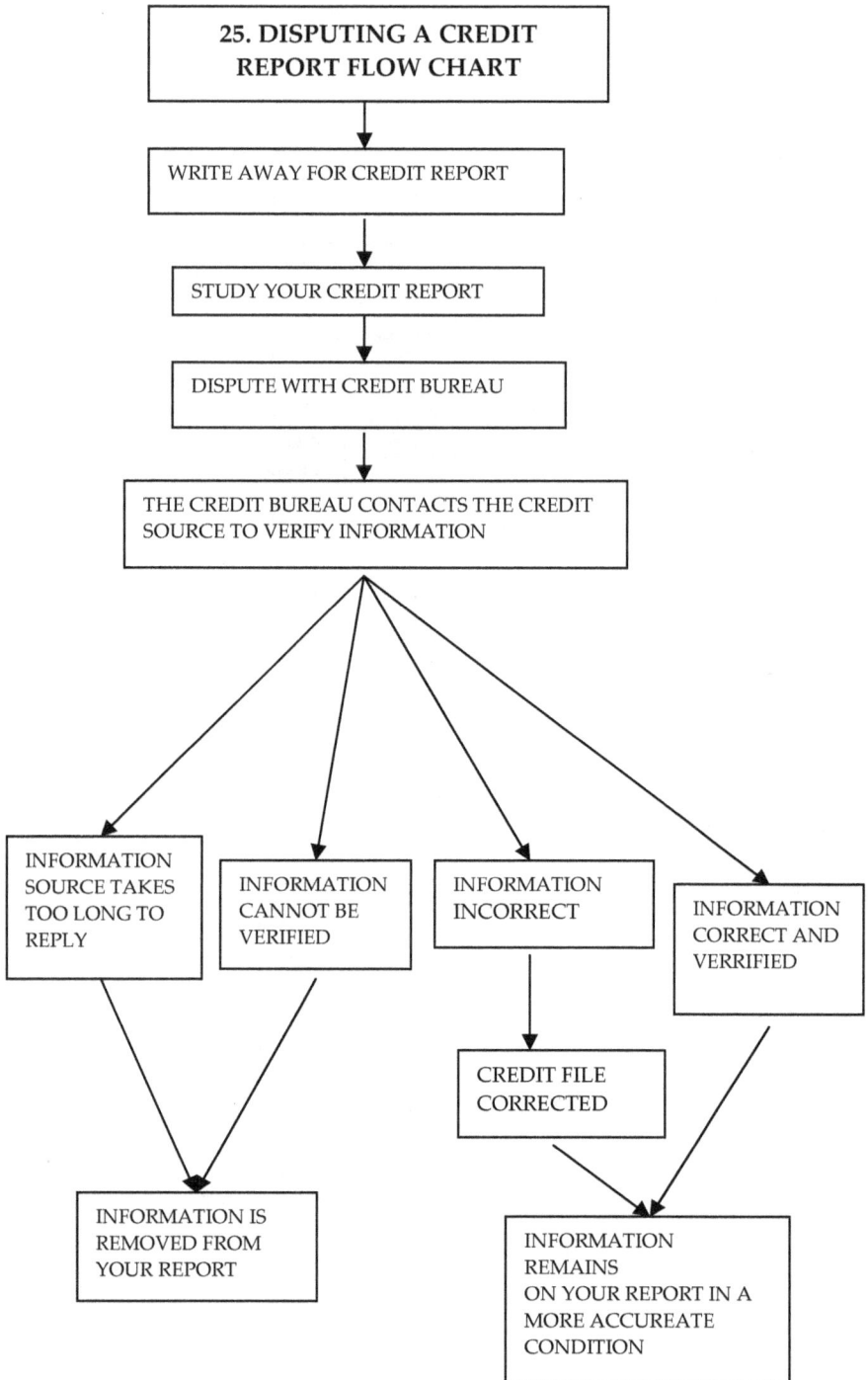

```
                  ┌─────────────────────────┐
                  │  25. DISPUTING A CREDIT  │
                  │   REPORT FLOW CHART      │
                  └─────────────────────────┘
                             │
                             ▼
                  ┌─────────────────────────┐
                  │ WRITE AWAY FOR CREDIT REPORT │
                  └─────────────────────────┘
                             │
                             ▼
                  ┌─────────────────────────┐
                  │ STUDY YOUR CREDIT REPORT │
                  └─────────────────────────┘
                             │
                             ▼
                  ┌─────────────────────────┐
                  │ DISPUTE WITH CREDIT BUREAU │
                  └─────────────────────────┘
                             │
                             ▼
        ┌────────────────────────────────────────┐
        │ THE CREDIT BUREAU CONTACTS THE CREDIT    │
        │ SOURCE TO VERIFY INFORMATION             │
        └────────────────────────────────────────┘
```

25. DISPUTING A CREDIT REPORT FLOW CHART

WRITE AWAY FOR CREDIT REPORT

STUDY YOUR CREDIT REPORT

DISPUTE WITH CREDIT BUREAU

THE CREDIT BUREAU CONTACTS THE CREDIT SOURCE TO VERIFY INFORMATION

INFORMATION SOURCE TAKES TOO LONG TO REPLY

INFORMATION CANNOT BE VERIFIED

INFORMATION INCORRECT

INFORMATION CORRECT AND VERRIFIED

CREDIT FILE CORRECTED

INFORMATION IS REMOVED FROM YOUR REPORT

INFORMATION REMAINS ON YOUR REPORT IN A MORE ACCUREATE CONDITION

PART II
REBUILDING YOUR CREDIT

26. ALL ABOUT LOANS

The best way to get a loan from a bank, trust company or other professional lender is by having collateral. If you have something tangible that you can use to put up against the loan, it is likely you will not have difficulty in obtaining a loan.

Most loans now, however, are "personal loans", in which your good name is the promise to repay. If you have "spoiled" your "good name" by repeatedly breaking your word to repay, you may have to go to a small loans company and offer collateral and pay a higher interest rate.

This is not to say that if your prospects of paying back the loan are dismal, a reputable bank won't outright refuse to lend you money, even if you do have sufficient collateral. It is always their option whether they lend us money or not. Reputable institutions do not want to foreclose on your home or take your car if you are in a tight bind to pay back a loan. The last thing a lender (except the odd blood sucker out there, yes they do exist) wants is to take property.

Usually, lending institutions lose money when they foreclose on a property or vehicle. Trust companies and banks are not in the used car business and they do not like to buy and sell houses except when economic conditions force them to.

The second best way to get a loan is if you have a co-signer with collateral. Some institutions do not presently permit co-signers. You may have to obtain a supplemental credit card from someone who has good credit and they will be first and solely responsible for payments. If your brother signs the loan as your co-signer and then you cannot pay your debt for whatever reason, it is not your home that will be forfeited but your brother's, or not your car but your mother's, or whatever belonging to whomever you have convinced you would pay the loan back. I suspect this would make for a rather troubled Thanksgiving with your family.

27.   FINANCE COMPANIES

Finance companies will sometimes make loans in circumstances where banks will refuse them, but the interest rates of finance companies are higher than at banks and the name of a finance company on your credit report is a flag to other credit granters that you have had difficulty acquiring credit. Be careful of the "buy now pay later" sales techniques used by some of the large furniture stores. If you do not pay within the specified time, often the store will sell your debt for the furniture to a finance company and even if you have previously had a good credit rating, the inclusion of a finance company on your credit report does not look good. Also, the debt at the furniture store is sometimes immediately written up by a finance company, not the retailer, so read the small print carefully.

28.   LEASE TO OWN

For those who desperately need to acquire a T.V. set, D.V.D. player or furniture and cannot wait to collect the cash to purchase these goods there is always the prospect of lease to own.   There are a number of companies who will, at relatively high rates, lease you furnishings and some of these contracts do leave you with ownership after the contract expires. But remember, read the fine print and watch out for finance companies!

29. CAR AND LIGHT TRUCK LEASERS OF LAST RESORT

The same as in furniture and appliance leasing there is also a "last resort" for car or light truck leasing. If you have not cleared a bad credit rating or have declared bankruptcy within the past seven years you will not be able to get a vehicle by the normal methods.

You might have to resort to what is sarcastically known in the auto industry as "roach leasing". The leasers in these instances charge horrendous rates for older vehicles; however, if you have no other alternative you are at their mercy. Just remember, as with anything in life, the deal you get will depend on how much you shop around.

30. DIFFERENT KIND OF LOAN APPLICATION TECHNIQUE

At some point you are going to find you have done everything you can to correct past problems with your credit rating. When all the letter writing and negotiating is over, it will be time to start re-building your credit rating from scratch. All the negatives possible have been removed and you have a clean, or near clean, slate and must start to add to it new, positive information.

The problem you will face once you have cleaned your credit rating is that you still won't have the positive comments necessary to get credit. It is possible, however, even easy to re-build a new, strong credit rating from scratch. The best way to prove to potential credit granters that you can pay them back regularly is to add a few loans to your credit rating that you have been, or are in the process of, paying back regularly. The problem is, as you know, few will loan you money before you get your credit rating rebuilt.

You might have to shop around but there are banks, trust, and insurance companies that will allow you to take out a loan against your IRA (Individual Retirement Account). The way this works is that the institution will loan you the money to take out the IRA. and they in turn will hold the IRA as collateral for the loan. Often the loan must be in the form of a term deposit. They will have all the money in their own vault (or wherever) you can't beat that for secured collateral.

Any other small loan that you do pay off without problems will assist your credit report. Most banks now hesitate to make $1,000 loans and will suggest the use of a credit card, either yours or a friend/family member's for small amounts. Talk to the bank, discuss the matter with them. Ask how much they will loan you, don't be dishonest, but don't be too quick to proclaim your past problems either.

The IRA loan is an immediate way to start rebuilding your credit record without the need for other collateral or a guarantor and you are not likely to be turned down. Another bonus of this type of loan is you will be opening a savings account that will be building as you pay off the loan. Once the loan is paid off you will have money in the bank although it will be best to leave it there for retirement. If you must cash in the IRA before you reach the age of 59.5 years you will have to pay the income tax on this money. Your agent at the institution where you take the loan will be qualified to brief you on this. But the benefits are fantastic; when you first take out the IRA your tax refund will swell by a good amount. The exact amount will depend on other financial commitments (dependents, income, etc.)

If you are 59.5 years old, you can withdraw your money out of your IRA without paying a penalty. If you withdraw prior to that time you will pay a penalty of 10%.

There are only two exceptions to avoid penalties when withdrawing money from your IRA prior to age 59.5 years.

1. If you are over 55 years old and are leaving your employer;

2. You become disabled.

Remember that even if you are eligible to withdraw your own money, you will still have to pay income tax (although not a penalty) on the amount withdrawn. The only exception is if it goes directly into an Individual Retirement Account (IRA) or if it goes directly into another plan sponsored by an employer.

31. IMPORTANCE OF CREDIT CARDS

Credit cards are so important in our modern society that many would argue that big brother is truly upon us. With banks recording record profits year after year, they continue to charge outrageous interest rates from anyone who cannot repay 100% of their monthly bill.

It is a modern injustice that a man or woman who is responsible and prefers to pay cash for goods received cannot easily rent a car, reserve a hotel room or make an airplane reservation. This decent soul cannot order many goods over the telephone or internet without needing to get a friend to order for them. This is not right! Unfortunately, there is not much we can do against the big and powerful banks and other financial institutions. It is their park and their ball we are playing with, so if we want to play in their games we have to play by their rules.

32. TYPES OF CREDIT CARDS

32.1 NORMAL

Most of us are familiar with the normal type of credit card, one which is granted to those whose credit ratings pass the acid test of credit scrutiny. With these cards you are billed monthly for charges and if there is **any** unpaid amount left on your bill after you have made your payment (by required date) the full original amount is subject to interest for the entire month's maximum balance.

Not only are these interest charges immediate but they are also compounded, so if your card company charges you ten percent interest on your unpaid balance of $100 this month, next month you will owe interest on $110., and the month after that your amount due will be $110 plus the next interest payment of $11, or $110 plus $11 = $121 and so on and on forever or until you make not only the **minimum** but also the **complete** payment. Not only is the interest charge very high but if your monthly bill is for $100 and you pay $90 you will be charged interest (by most of these companies) on the full orriginal amount of $100.

32.2 SUPPLEMENTARY

Supplementary credit cards differ from the normal card only in that they are a second (or third) card on one account. If, for example, your husband or wife has a credit card with ABC Finance and you don't have an account with them, it is likely that the company would be willing to issue you a card in your name but billed to your spouse's account (or your parent's account, etc.). This system will help you to make your purchases with greater convenience but will do little to build up your credit file because the cards are still billed to the other person's name.

32.3 CO-SIGNED

If you want to use another person's good credit to help you to get a credit card that will assist you in rebuilding your credit file, try to get a CO-SIGNED credit card account. In this instance the friend or spouse still lends you their good reputation and does still take responsibility if you should default in your payments but you will have your very own account, a card with your name on it and the freedom that comes with it. (Just be careful to use it only if you can pay it!)

32.4   SECURED

There may not be someone available to either give you a supplemental credit card or perhaps sign for a co-signed credit card for you, or your credit situation may be such that it is unwise or difficult for you to ask such a favour. In these cases you can almost always get a SECURED credit card.

This type of credit card works almost the reverse from all the other types. Instead of buying on credit and paying the bill when it comes in, you maintain a balance in the bank or trust company and they debit your balance when you make a purchase.

You might wish to use money from your income tax refund (especially if you used the IRA technique discussed earlier) or you may wish to save the money on your own; however, with as little as $500 cash you can often convince a loans officer at a bank or trust company to issue you a credit card chargeable against this cash if it is deposited in an account in his or her bank. Remember, that if you run short of cash on the 12th of the month and dip into that account for $400 you will not be able to charge $125 against that account on the 14th, and this action would make your credit rating look even worse as well.

Several reputable <u>and many not reputable companies</u> offer secured credit cards. The bad ones have been in the news. But you can obtain a fair deal from many banks and savings and loan companies in most states.

32.5 CAMPAIGN

There are times when credit cards are easier to get than other times. If, for example ABC Department store has a CAMPAIGN under way to sign up a whole new group of credit card holders, it might be easier for you to get approval and to receive a credit card at that time than it would be a month earlier or later. You can often spot these canvassers at the entrances to stores asking those who pass by if they would like to apply for a credit card. Sometimes these people can be a nuisance but to you, they could be a way to start rebuilding your credit file.

These same canvassers often offer free gifts for just applying for the credit card, so go for it, collect your gift and apply for a credit card, even if you usually don't shop in that particular store you are at least working to get a better credit rating and it will be easier to get other credit cards after because you can use ABC Department Store as a reference (if you pay your bills on time).

33. FINANCE COMPANIES

There are a few things to remember about finance companies.

1) Finance companies usuallyo charge higher interest rates than banks, or Trust Companies, or Savings & Loan Associations or Thrifts;

2) Finance companies these days use almost exactly the same criteria for accepting or rejecting loan applicants as do banks;

3) Many loan granters view the presence of a

finance company on an applicant's credit file to imply that the applicant had no choice other than the use of a finance company;

4) Many large furniture companies with delayed payment options immediately sell loans to finance companies. So if you wish to "buy now but don't pay until September", or January or 2015 or whatever sales gimmick they will be using when you read this, just be aware that you may be dealing with XYZ Finance Company when you sign on the dotted line.

34.   CAR AND TRUCK FINANCING

It is often difficult for someone with an R-1 (excellent) credit rating to get a car loan on a used vehicle using the vehicle as collateral since the car <u>might</u> depreciate faster than the loan will be paid off, and a new car will <u>definitely</u> depreciate faster than the loan will be paid off.   The only reason the companies are as willing to loan money on new cars as easily as they do, is because this is such a large part of their loan business and even then they are particular to a fault as to whom they will or will not make the loan to.

If you require a vehicle and are unable to find one through the normal channels you might be eligible for a high risk lease.

35.   LOAN GRANTING CRITERIA

Item #36 (below) contains two examples of check sheets used to ascertain the reliability of a consumer and the likelihood of his or her being able and willing to pay back a loan. IN THE EYES OF CREDITORS, that is, not in our opinion. Obviously, there is no foolproof method for the creditors to know who will pay back a loan and who will not; however, these lists are some of their attempts at separating the good risks from the bad. Try going to bankrate.com and checking your credit rating. Bankrate also has economic computer software that will help you to determine the steps necessary to improve a less than optimum credit rating.

Go to:

http://www.bankrate.com/calculators/credit-score-fico-calculator.aspx

36.   NEGATIVE ITEMS ON A CREDIT APPLICATION

There is one list you should be familiar with and this may be the most important of all. If any of the following items appear on your credit application, you are in serious jeopardy of not getting any loans for any reason.

<u>LIST ONE</u>

1)   Bankruptcy;
2)   High debt to income;
3)   Foreigners without permanent status;
4)   Post office boxes;
5)   Frequent changes in address;
6)   Frequent changes in employment;
7)   Self Employed;

8) No telephone or not in applicant's name;
9) Unskilled labourer;
10) Poor paying prestige position;
11) Excessive number of credit cards, or revolving credit account;
12) Employers with un-verifiable telephone numbers;
13) No checking or savings account.

Some of the items on this list take work and help to rectify, some just take time, while others can usually be corrected easily and quickly, this last group includes

LIST TWO

1) Post office boxes;
2) Frequent changes in address;
3) Frequent changes in employment;
4) Self employed;
5) No telephone;
6) Excessive number of credit cards;
7) Un-verifiable telephone numbers of employers;
8) No checking or savings account.

There are numerous situations which will govern each of these items; the one which I will say a little more about is SELF EMPLOYMENT. You can keep on doing exactly what you have been doing if you so desire; however, give yourself a promotion,.Don't be Joe Smith, self employed electrician (and I know electricians who make lots of money) but be a person with position, Joe Smith, President, Manager, Foreman, Vice-President or just simply first class electrician for Joe Smith Electrical Contracting. The best bet; however, is to give your company a different name from yours.

37. IDENTITY THEFT

In 2004, it was estimated that over 10 million people were victims of identity theft. The number had dropped to 8.4 million in 2007. Protect yourself against identity theft, look for recently opened accounts or new addresses that are not familiar to you. These could be signs of identity theft.

Please do yourself a favour and go to your

computer, or a friend's computer if you don't have one and take a look at the following web sites.

eHow.com at:
http://www.ehow.com/about_4604203_many-people-affected-identity-theft.html#ixzz13qrNfFJJ

and also go to:

The Identity Theft Resource Center at:
http://www.idtheftcenter.org/

Identity theft occurs when someone else tries to fool lenders or other authorities into believing they are you in order to obtain your money either directly, through credit or to acquire your property, which they would generally sell quickly and then disappear with the proceeds. The identity thief will sometimes lease or buy vehicles, rent property or engage in more dangerous criminal activity. There are many well documented cases where identity thieves have taken over the identity of another person and have sold expensive property and have then disappeared with the proceeds.

In order to protect you from identity theft follow these suggestions from Equifax:

- Monitor your credit reports;
- Do not carry more credit cards or I.D. than you require, either locally or internationally;
- Do not carry credit cards with your cheques;
- If you misplace or lose your cheque book, call your bank immediately;
- Always sign your credit cards in permanent ink immediately as your receive them;
- When making a purchase, keep your credit cards in view at all times;
- Do not sign blank charge slips;
- Always take your receipts, if you wish to destroy them, do it privately;
- Do not repeat your account number so that it can be overheard;
- Only give your I.D. and credit card numbers over the phone on calls which you have initiated;
- Do not provide your account numbers over the telephone to

someone who has called you and claims to represent the card company or the police. Card companies will already have this information and the polices do not do this;

- If your Social Security Number card is lost or stolen:

    i. File a complaint with the Federal Trade Commission(1-877-ID-THEFT or 1-877-438-4338);

    ii. File an online complaint with the Internet Crime Complaint Center at http://www.ic3.gov;

    iii. Check your Social Security records (call toll-free 1-800-772-1213; TTY 1-800-325-0778) to ensure your income is calculated correctly;

- If your drivers license is lost or stolen, report it immediately to the police and the local D.O.T.

(Department of Transport) office;

- Do not respond to any emails stating they are from the bank requesting personal information (account number, password, etc., Banks and Trust companies do not send out this kind of questionnaire.)

Be careful with your credit and debit card statements. Check your statements as soon as they arrive, confirm all charges are legitimate. Keep your statements safe; shred them after your review of them, the information in them is private and confidential. When your credit cards or bank cards are lost or stolen:

- Have a list of the cards, numbers and expiration dates in a safe place (not with the cards). This can be used to quickly alert the bank and charge companies of missing cards;

- Call all the card companies as soon as you realize the cards are missing. Most cards can be re-activated later if you discover them under the dresser.

Finally, computer advertisers may use "cookies" to gather information on you.

Visit http://www.networkadvertising.org to learn more.

38.   PARTING NOTES

By now you certainly have a much better understanding of credit and how it works than most people do, try to use this knowledge wisely. Good credit, once earned, is easy to maintain and a joy to employ. You deserve good credit as much as anyone does, go the extra bit and make the extra effort; I'll be rooting for you all the way.

Good luck and good credit,
Bill Colucci

39. QUESTIONS ON CREDIT REPAIR CYCLE

1) What is another name for a credit reporting agency?

2) What is the largest credit reporting agency in the U.S.A.?

3) When denied credit you have the right to:

   1. Complain
   2. Telephone the Federal Trade Commission
   3. To know if a credit reporting agency was used in making the decision to deny you credit and if so which one

4) When writing a credit reporting agency for you credit file your letter should include:

   (i)   Your name
   ii)   Your address
   (iii) Your previous address
   (iv)   Your present and previous employers
   (v)   Your date of birth
   (vi)   All of the above

5)   For correcting your credit problems
        a help is:

        (i)   The Consumer Reporting Act
        (ii)   The Fair Credit Reporting Act
        (iii)   The Bankruptcy Act

6)   True or False. The following
        businesses and financial institutions
        report credit information back to the
        credit bureaus.

        (i) Home mortgages
        T___ F___
        (ii) Most oil companies
        T___ F___
        (iii) Insurance companies
        T___ F___
        (iv) Major credit cards
        T___ F___
        (v) Major department stores
        T___ F___

7)   What is the best or most desirable R
        - rating you could
        have on your credit file?

        R - 9?
        R - 1?
        R - 100?

8)   Fill in the blank:

Credit is generally damaged if you have an R - rating over R..........

9) A credit granter, when considering you for credit might take into consideration which of the following:

(i)   Your credit report
(ii) Your bank records
(iii) Length of employment
(iv) Length of time at your present and previous addresses
(v)   Your income
(vi) All of the above

10) True or False?
The Fair Credit Reporting act makes no reference to what information can legally be on your credit file.

11) True or False?
The best way to proceed in getting the assistance of a consumer reporting agency to help you to correct errors on your credit file is to be tough and demand immediate assistance!

12) True or False?

Make all correspondence with the credit bureau look as professional and as much like a legal office's correspondence as possible.

13) Put the following in their proper order.

    i)   Send a follow up letter

    ii)   Send in one dispute letter for 3 or less items

    iii)   Depending on the outcome of your dispute, either send in your next dispute or try re-submitting from another city, all the time learning to "play the game" better

    iv)   Wait four weeks

    v)   Either re-mail a dispute letter or calmly wait for action on your dispute (no more than seven weeks).

14) Poor credit can affect your credit rating for up to...

(i) 3 years...

(ii) 10 years...

(iii) 7 year....

15) You can often negotiate directly with creditors because their main interest is usually...

(i) Revenge

(ii) Getting their money

(iii) Protecting other businesses from bad debts

(iv) They enjoy seeing those in debt suffer

16) You should employ legal action...

i) Immediately against all concerned?

ii) To sue the credit bureau if they give out a bad file on you?

iii) As a last resort only?

17) Negotiating with a creditor before a report goes in to the bureau on you is... (Check one)

i)   Useless?

ii)   Frivolous?

iii)   A good way to limit damage
        to your credit file?

(iv) The only way to proceed?

(18)   A consumer statement is... (Check
        one)

i)   A last resort?

ii)   The easiest and most
        available defense of
        your credit history?

iii)   Absolutely useless?

19) What is the best way to get a loan?

20) The "buy now and pay later" sales pitch
    Popular today is:

    1) Usually a good deal
    2) Always a good deal
    3) Can create problems
    4) Is often not what it seems

21) If you take out an IRA for collateral you
    may have to shop around, would this

be worth the trouble?

22) AN IRA loan requires:

    1) Separate collateral
    2) A top credit rating
    3) A co-signer
    4) None of the above

23) Having a credit card is necessary or at least helpful in obtaining:

    1) Hotel reservations
    2) Airline reservations
    3) Cashing a check
    4) All of the above

24) The interest charged on most bank cards is:

    1) Nominal
    2) A little high
    3) Criminal
    4) Very expensive

25) Describe in your own words:

    1) Supplementary
    2) Co-signed
    3) Secured
    4) Campaign credit cards

26) The appearance of your credit rating will be better if you list yourself as:

    1) An employee of a company (your own company included)

    2) A managing partner of your own company

    3) A sole proprietor

27) Now that you have read the right material you will:

    1) Improve your credit rating and let it slip back to bad again?

    2) Forget about it and do nothing?

    3) Improve your credit rating and keep it good?

40. ANSWERS TO CREDIT REPAIR QUESTIONS

1) Credit Bureau
2) Equifax
3) (iii)
4) (vi)
5) (ii)
6) (i) T
   (ii) T
   (iii) T
   (iv) T
   (v) T
7) R 1
8) R 2
9) (vi)
10) False
11) False
12) False
13) (ii), (iv), (i), (v), (iii)
14) (iii)
15) (ii)
16) (iii)
17) (iii) or (iv)
18) (ii)
19) Collateral
20) 3 or 4 - these deals can create problems and usually have terms attached that you should avoid
21) Definitely yes!
22) 4 - none of the above
23) 4 - all of the above

24) 4 - very expensive
25) These are your words, read chapter one and check for   how accurate you are.
26)(1), an employee of a company, your own included.
27)Hopefully (3), improve your credit rating & keep it good.

www.ingramcontent.com/pod-product-compliance
Lightning Source LLC
Chambersburg PA
CBHW022029090426
42739CB00006BA/356